Totally Lent!

A KID'S JOURNEY TO EASTER 2009

Mary Behe and Margaret Savitskas

Edited by Jean Larkin

Pflaum Publishing Group
Dayton, OH

About the Authors

Mary Behe has been involved in catechesis for many years. Her ministry has included being a classroom catechist, Director of Religious Education, and a member of RCIA and RCIT teams.

Margaret Savitskas has a wide variety of experience in religious education. She has worked in publishing and has written children's books, textbooks, and teacher guides. She loves working with children and is currently Director of Children's Catechesis at St. Elizabeth Ann Seton Parish in Fort Wayne, IN. Margaret holds degrees in English and Education and is working toward a Master's Degree in Theology at the University of Notre Dame.

Graphic design by Linda Becker and Ellen Wright
Cover and interior illustrations by Doug Jones, www.dougjonesart.com

Many of the Scripture references in this book are paraphrased, based on the translation from the *New Revised Standard Version Bible: Catholic Edition*. Any direct quotations contained herein are from the *New Revised Standard Version Bible: Catholic Edition* copyright © 1993 and 1989 by the Division of Christian Education of the National Council of the Churches of Christ in the U.S.A. Used by permission. All rights reserved.

Pflaum Publishing Group
2621 Dryden Rd., Suite 300
Dayton, OH 45439
800-543-4383
pflaum.com

ISBN 978-1-933178-98-1

What Are You Doing for Lent?

The Church teaches us to do penance during Lent. This means to do something good to make up for our sins. It means to make sacrifices. A sacrifice is an offering to God given with love.

Many people give up something as a sacrifice during Lent. That's fine if it is something that gets in the way of a person's relationship with Jesus. But if you give up candy and keep on being mean to your brother, what good does that do? It would be better to give up being mean to your brother!

Lent is a time to do something that will help you grow closer to God and will let the life of Christ grow in you. You might pray more, be more helpful to others, or do your chores without complaining. You get the idea.

Totally Lent! will help you keep track of your spiritual growth throughout the next six weeks. On pages 32 and 33, there is a drawing of a sunflower. This sunflower will be your growth chart. Every Saturday you will make note of how much you have grown.

Take some time now to think about what you will do this Lent. Write your promise for Lent in the space on page 32.

Today's Gospel: Matthew 6:1-6, 16-18

Jesus said, "Beware of practicing your piety in front of others so they can see you" (6:1).

Today, the priest or minister used blessed ashes to make a cross on your forehead. The ashes remind us that life on earth is only for a while. Now is the time to turn to God, be sorry for sins, and try to do better.

After hearing or reading today's Gospel, choose the correct ending for what Jesus said about praying, fasting, and giving alms.

When you pray

1. Do ___B___

2. Do not ___a___

    A. Stand up in public so everyone will notice.

    B. Go to your room and close the door.

When you fast

3. Do ___B___

4. Do not ___a___

    A. Look gloomy so everyone knows what you are doing.

    B. Look happy so no one knows what you are doing.

When you give alms

5. Do ___a___

6. Do not ___B___

    A. Keep your good deeds secret.

    B. Call attention to yourself.

Today you may see someone who doesn't know what the ashes on your forehead mean. Take time to explain what Lent is about.

Thursday after Ash Wednesday— February 26

Today's Gospel: Luke 9:22-25

Jesus said to his disciples: "If any of you want to become my followers, let them deny themselves and take up their cross daily and follow me" (9:23).

You deny yourself whenever you do anything that puts other people first. Two examples are when you play the game your friend wants to play or you give up your free time to read to your little brother. That is not always easy, is it?

If any of you want to become my followers, let them deny themselves and take up their cross daily and follow me.

1. Trace this cross pattern on construction paper.

2. Cut around the outside of the cross shape.

3. Print Jesus' words from above on the cross.

4. Fold each square toward the center to make a cube shape.

5. Tape the cube closed.

Keep the cross cube where it will remind you to follow Jesus daily.

Friday after Ash Wednesday—
February 27

Today's Gospel: Matthew 9:14-15

Jesus said, "The wedding guests cannot be sad when the bridegroom is with them. The days will come when he is taken away. Then they will fast" (9:15).

Lent is the time we prepare for the day when Jesus "is taken away." It is a time for sacrifices. Sometimes a choice might look like a sacrifice but really isn't.

Check the choice that makes these examples true sacrifices.

1. **You love shrimp. You have a choice of two menu items this Friday. Choose one.**

   ☐ **Shrimp**
   ☒ **Macaroni and cheese**

2. **You gave up video games for Lent. A friend has a new game and asks you to play. What do you do?**

   ☒ **You say "no." You explain to your friend about Lent.**
   ☐ **You say "yes." You decide it would be rude to refuse.**

3. **Your neighbor asks you to help her in her yard. She will pay you.**

   ☐ **You help her and save the money for a new bike.**
   ☒ **You help her, save half the money, and give half to the poor.**

Jesus, accept the sacrifice I make today as a small sign of my love for you. Amen.

37 Saturday after Ash Wednesday— February 28

Today's Gospel: Luke 5:27-32

Jesus said, "Those who are well have no need of a physician. I have come to call not the righteous but sinners to repentance" (5:31-32).

When we sin, our souls get sick. Jesus heals us and returns us to spiritual health. Solve this puzzle to discover how we receive his healing. Using the clues, fill in this grid. Then *sound* out the words of the answer and write it in the space below.

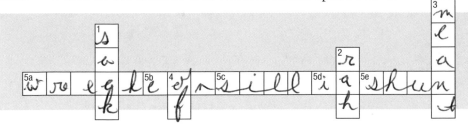

1. A tackle on the quarterback before he hands off the ball; or you might carry your lunch in one

2. Half of a cheer

3. "I said what I _____, and I _____ what I said."

4. Two-letter preposition that rhymes with love

5. a. If two ships collide, there is a ship_____
   b. A scam artist is also called a _____ man
   c. A sunny spot for a plant is a window_____
   d. The fifth letter of the alphabet
   e. Refuse to speak to or look at someone

The *Sacrament of Reconciliation*

Jesus, I am sorry for all my sins. Thank you for being my healer when I need it. Help me to avoid sin and to stay healthy. Amen.

Did You Know?

Lent comes from the Anglo-Saxon word for "lengthen." The Anglo-Saxons watched the sun, moon, and stars to judge the time of year. When the sun shone longer and longer each day and the weather got warmer and warmer, it was the time of "lengthening" days. It was also the time when birds laid eggs, when flowers bloomed, and when baby animals were born. It was a time of new life! It was the season of spring.

When is your birthday? <u>December 5</u>
Is it the same month and day every year?   ☒ Yes ☐ No
Is it always on the same day of the week?   ☐ Yes ☒ No

When is Christmas? <u>December 25</u>
Is it the same month and day every year?   ☒ Yes ☐ No
Is it always on the same day of the week?   ☐ Yes ☒ No

When is the 4th of July? Ha ha, trick question!

When is Easter? <u>Sunday</u>
Is it the same month and day every year?   ☐ Yes ☒ No
Is it always on the same day of the week?   ☒ Yes ☐ No

Now, that's interesting! Unlike your birthday, Christmas, and the 4th of July, Easter is celebrated on a *different day each year*. Unlike your birthday, Christmas, and the 4th of July, Easter is always celebrated on the *same day of the week—Sunday*.

Why? The Church wanted to celebrate the resurrection of Jesus at the time of year it happened. The Gospels tell us that Jesus celebrated the Passover on the night before he died. On the third day, he rose from the dead. So the date of Easter was based on the time of Passover. There are different ways to calculate that day, but one is this: *Easter is the first Sunday after the first full moon after the first day of spring.* Got that? It is *always* on Sunday—the first day of our week!

The Season of Lent

Lent is the most solemn season of the Church year. It is a time for prayer and sacrifice. The liturgy of Lent shows this mood.

During Lent, the joyful word *Alleluia* is missing from the liturgy. Alleluia, which means "Glory to God," returns on Easter Sunday.

Bury the Alleluia

Here is something you can do today. On a sheet of paper, write the word ALLELUIA. Color it with bright colors and decorate it with glitter or sequins or ribbons or pompoms. It should look really festive. Then put your ALLELUIA in a brown paper bag or box. Shove the bag or box way back in the corner of your closet or under your bed.

Remember, during Lent we have to go way down deep into ourselves. We have to look inside and find our bad habits and get rid of them.

First Monday of Lent—March 2

Today's Gospel: Matthew 25:31-46

When the day of judgment comes, Jesus said he would separate the good from the bad people. He would invite the good people into his Father's kingdom and tell them, "I was hungry and you gave me food" (25:31-35).

Design a new coin based on today's Gospel. Draw ideas for both sides of the coin.

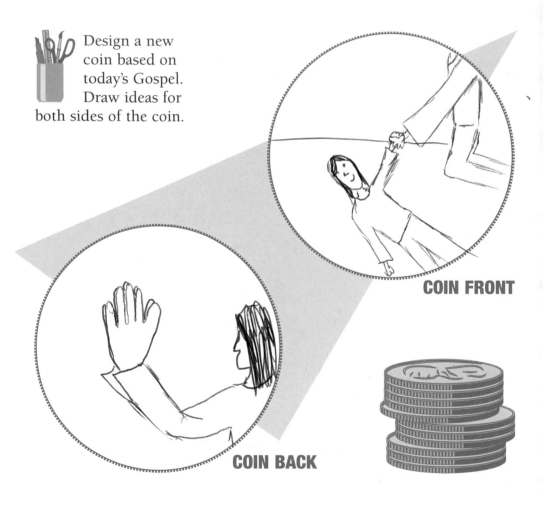

COIN FRONT

COIN BACK

 Lord, when was it that we saw you hungry and gave you food? "If you did it to one of the least among you, you did it for me." (See Matthew 25:37-40.)

Today's Gospel: Matthew 6:7-15

Jesus said, "When you are praying, do not heap up empty phrases…for your Father knows what you need before you ask him" (6:7, 8).

It was no mistake that Jesus said the Father knows what you *need* and not what you *want*. St. Basil said, "The bread you do not use is the bread of the hungry; the garment hanging in your closet is the clothing of the naked; the shoes you do not wear are the shoes of someone who is barefoot; the money you keep locked away is the money of the poor."

 Decide how you might act on St. Basil's words this week.

Do you buy snacks for yourself? How could you help the hungry this week?

No. Give money to church.

Are there clothes or shoes in your closet that you don't need? How could you help the naked this week?

Yes. Donate them to House of Hope.

Are you saving money for something you want but don't need? How could you help the poor this week?

Yes. Give them that $.

 Today is the feast of St. Katherine Drexel. She used her wealth to build schools and missions for African Americans and Native Americans in the USA. St. Katherine Drexel, pray for us.

First Wednesday of Lent—
March 4

Today's Gospel: Luke 11:29-32

Jesus said to the people, "This generation is an evil generation; it asks for a sign, but no sign will be given to it except the sign of Jonah" (11:29).

God told Jonah to go to Nineveh and tell the people to repent. Jonah really didn't want to save the people of Nineveh because they were enemies of his people. So he hopped a ship going in the opposite direction! (Read Jonah 1—3 to see how this reluctant prophet became a great sign to the people of Nineveh. It's kind of a fishy story. ☺)

 Beginning with the S, write every other letter on the lines inside the puzzle until you've used all the letters. You'll discover the point Jesus made today about Jonah.

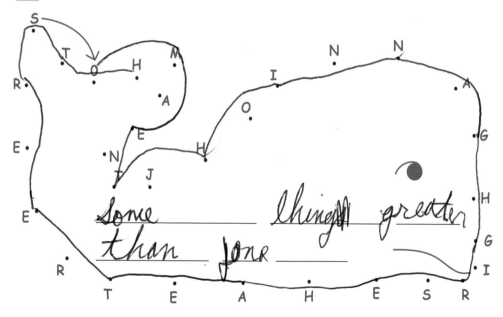

Some   things greater
than   Jone

Now, beginning with the S again, connect each letter to the one next to it, dot-to-dot. Now, do you remember Jonah?

 Lord Jesus, help me to follow your will even when I am reluctant. Amen.

First Thursday of Lent—March 5

Today's Gospel: Matthew 7:7-12

Jesus said, "Do to others as you would have them do to you" (7:12).

The answer to each of these clues is a number from 0-12. Each number stands for a letter. Once you have answered the clue, put the number's corresponding letter on the line in the ruler.

Ruler	Clue
0 __T__	How many Gospels are in the Bible? __4__ = O
1 __H__	How many sacraments are there? __7__ = E
2 __E__	How many decades are there in a rosary? __5__ = L
3 __G__	For Catholics 14 and older, how many servings of meat are allowed on Good Friday? __0__ = T
4 __O__	How many Gods are there in the Trinity? __1__ = H
5 __L__	How many commandments did God give Moses on Mt. Sinai? __10__ = U
6 __D__	How many apostles were there? __12__ = E
7 __E__	How many persons are there in the Trinity? __3__ = G
8 __N__	How many commandments are the "Great commandments"? __2__ = E
9 __R__	How many days are there in a novena? __9__ = R
10 __U__	How many letters are there in the word for how Jesus died? __11__ = L
11 __L__	How many weeks are in Lent? __6__ = D
12 __E__	How many Beatitudes are there? __8__ = N

Now read the letters vertically to find the name for the advice Jesus gave in today's Gospel.

Jesus, help me always to treat others fairly, respectfully, and with kindness. Amen.

Today's Gospel: Matthew 5:20-26

Jesus said, "When you are offering your gift at the altar, if you remember that your brother or sister has something against you, leave your gift at the altar and go first and reconcile with your brother or sister. Then come and offer your gift" (5:23-24).

- You are giving up TV for Lent, but your brother is not. You pester him and make noise while he's watching TV. Is God pleased with your Lenten sacrifice? ☺ ●

- Your family has a Lenten giving box on the kitchen table. You put your leftover pennies in it at day's end and put the rest of your coins in your pocket. Is God pleased with your almsgiving? ☺ ●

- You promised to keep your room clean during Lent. One day your mom asks you to clean the sink and mirror in the bathroom. You yell, "I never said I'd do that!" Is God pleased with your Lenten promise? ☺ ●

Keep a smile on your face today. Notice how people react. Did you get funny looks? Did anyone ask what you were up to?

Lord, help me to bring happiness through laughter, kind words, and a smile to those I meet each day. Amen.

First Saturday of Lent—March 7

Today's Gospel: Matthew 5:43-48

Jesus said, "Love your enemies and pray for your persecutors" (5:43).

Dominic takes your snack every day. Jesus said you should love and pray for Dominic. Do you?

Sarah told Jennifer a lie about you. Jesus said you should love and pray for Sarah. Do you?

Helena called you a name and now everyone is calling you that name. Jesus said you should love and pray for Helena. Do you?

Joe pushed you on purpose during a basketball game. You twisted your ankle. Jesus said you should love and pray for Joe. Do you?

"Love and pray for your enemies" is one of the most difficult things Jesus told us to do. Love and pray for people who are mean to us? who tell lies about us? who bully us? How does Jesus expect us to do that?

Arrange these words in order and you'll see what Jesus expects of us.

Heavenly • Be • Your • Is • Father • Perfect • As • Perfect

Be perfect as your Heavenly Father is perfect.

🌻 **How Much Have You Grown?**
Turn to pages 32 and 33. Read your Promise for Lent. How are you doing so far? On the space for Week 1, write about a sacrifice you made this week.

Did You Know?

The Dogwood Tree

Dogwood trees bloom in the woods each spring near the time of Easter. They are small, slender trees. Somewhere, someone looked closely at the blossom, and saw reminders of the passion of Jesus.

Each blossom is made up of four white petals in the shape of a cross. Each petal is touched with a reddish-brown mark, as if it had been wounded. The center of the flower resembles the crown of thorns, and it is bright red, representing the blood of Christ.

Perhaps because of the petals, a legend about the dogwood tree has been passed down. The Bible doesn't tell us what kind of wood was used to make the cross of Jesus. But the story goes that, in the time of Jesus, the dogwood tree grew tall and strong, and its wood was chosen to make the cross of Jesus.

Jesus saw how sad the tree was and promised that the dogwood would never again grow large enough to be used to make a cross. People of faith look at the dogwood tree and remember the suffering of Jesus.

Color the dogwood blossom as it is described in the story.

Lenten Legends

The Sand Dollar

The sand dollar is a sea creature that lives partly buried in sand. It is found in shallow coastal waters in many parts of the world. If you go for a walk on the beach after a storm, you may find the white shell or skeleton of a sand dollar.

The shell is beautiful, with fine designs on both sides. The story goes that Christ left the sand dollar for the apostles to help them teach people about him.

A sand dollar has five holes that represent the wounds of Christ. On one side of the shell is a design that looks something like an Easter lily. At the center of the flower is the star of Bethlehem.

On the other side of the sand dollar you can see the tracing of a poinsettia flower, another reminder of Christmas. When you break open the shell, you will release five small white teeth. These are said to be doves that will spread good will and peace.

Draw on the sand dollar the designs that are described in the story.

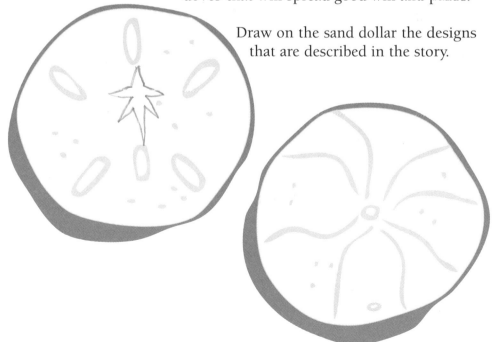

Today's Gospel: Luke 6:36-38

Jesus said, "The measure you give will be the measure you get back"
(6:38).

Today is the feast of St. Frances of Rome. She gave a large measure of her life to helping those in need. To read her story, fill in the missing words. Then circle them in the puzzle.

Frances lived long ago in the city of Rome. She was the mother of *three* children. Her husband was a *rich* man. Frances had an *easy poor* life. But she knew that everything she had came from *jewels God*. Frances sold her *jewels* and gave alms to the *poor*. When war and

G	R	A	I	N	W	I	S	W
E	N	H	P	P	N	D	O	I
N	L	G	E	O	A	R	U	N
E	R	I	L	O	R	O	P	E
R	I	V	E	R	I	D	A	A
O	C	R	J	E	W	E	L	S
S	H	D	N	W	T	A	A	Y
I	I	K	E	Y	A	T	C	Y
T	H	R	E	E	E	H	E	O
Y	G	O	D	C	K	K	N	E

famine hit the city, Frances worked harder for those in *need*. Her father-in-law complained about her *generosity* and took away the *key* to the storeroom. When he saw that the *grain* bin and the *wine* barrel were still full, he gave the key back to Frances. When the Tiber *River* flooded, a plague caused sickness and *death*. Frances set up a *soup* kitchen and invited homeless people to live in her big *palace*.

Word List

death	God	key	poor	soup
generosity	grain	need	rich	three
easy	jewels	palace	River	wine

Father, through St. Frances, you gave good things to people in need. Help me to give whatever I can when people need help. Amen.

Second Tuesday of Lent— March 10

Today's Gospel: Matthew 23:1-12

Jesus was talking to his disciples about the Pharisees. "They do all their deeds to be seen by others; for they make their phylacteries broad and their fringes long" (23:5-6).

During prayers, Jewish men wore phylacteries on their foreheads and left arms. These were little boxes that contained verses of Scripture. They also sewed tassels onto the corners of their head coverings to remind them of God's commandments.

Jesus said they made the phylacteries wider and the fringes longer than necessary to call attention to themselves instead of to God.

 What do you wear to remind you of God?

My Miraculous Medal

What is your attitude toward the things you wear? Do you care too much about having the "right" clothes?

I put on whatever's there. No.

Today, thank your parents for the clothes they provide for you. Be happy with what you have instead of wanting new stuff to show off.

 Did you know that actions can be prayers? If you act with love and unite your action to the work of Jesus, your act will be a prayer. Give it a try.

Second Wednesday of Lent— March 11

Today's Gospel: Matthew 20:17-28

On the way to Jerusalem, Jesus took his apostles aside and told them exactly what was going to happen to him when they got there. "The Son of Man will be handed over to the chief priests and scribes, and they will condemn him to death; then they will hand him over to the Gentiles to be mocked and flogged and crucified; and on the third day he will be raised" (20:18-19).

The apostles were clueless. They practically ignored what Jesus said about his suffering and rising. Instead, they argued about who would sit closest to him when he came into his kingdom!

If Jesus had had a cell phone, he could have text messaged the apostles and maybe he would have gotten their attention! Using this phone, decode the message he gave them.

Watch out! This can be tricky. Most numbers stand for multiple letters. To help you, some of the letters have been filled in.

(If you can't figure it out, reread today's Gospel.)

WHOEVER
9 4 6 3 8 3 7

WISHES TO
9 4 7 4 3 7 8 6

BE FIRST
2 3 3 4 7 7 8

AMONG
2 6 6 6 4

YOU
9 6 8

MUST BE
6 8 7 8 2 3

YOUR
9 6 8 7

SERVANT.
7 3 7 8 2 6 8

1	2 ABC	3 DEF
4 GHI	5 JKL	6 MNO
7 PQRS	8 TUV	9 WXYZ
*	0	#

Jesus, help me always to pay attention to the needs of others. Amen.

Second Thursday of Lent—March 12

Today's Gospel: Luke 16:19-31

Jesus told a story about a rich man who ignored a poor man as he lay starving outside the rich man's gate. Both men died. The poor man went to heaven, and the rich man went to hell. He cried out to Father Abraham for help but was told, "Remember that, during your life, you had all good things, and this poor man had none. Now he is comforted, and you are in agony. There is nothing anyone can do for you now" (16:19-26).

Do you ever get so caught up in your own stuff that you don't see when others need help? Spend ten minutes quietly observing the people around you at home.

This is what I see.

People doing homework

This is what I hear.

humming, yelling

This is what I can do to help someone today.

help John w/ his homework

God be in my head, and in my understanding.
God be in my eyes, and in my looking.
God be in my mouth, and in my speaking.
God be in my heart, and in my thinking.
God be at my end, and at my departing. (Sarum Primer, 1538)

Today's Gospel: Matthew 21:33-43, 45-46

Jesus said, "The kingdom of God will be given to a people that produces the fruits of the kingdom" (21:43).

Today's Gospel was the parable of the vineyard owner whose tenants refused to allow the owner to collect his fruit. They killed everyone he sent to get his property. They even killed the man's own son. As with most of Jesus' parables, he taught lessons to those who listened. If we are to belong to the kingdom of God, we must produce the fruits of God's kingdom. What are those fruits?

Fill in the missing letters of the words in these grapes to discover what some of those fruits are.

JUSTICE   KINDNESS   PEACE   LOVE   CHARITY   GOODNESS   HOPE   JOY   FAITH   PATIENCE

Almighty God, I want to belong to your kingdom. Help me to live like one of your children and heirs. Help me never to reject your ways. Amen.

Second Saturday of Lent— March 14

Today's Gospel: Luke 15:1-3, 11-32

Jesus told a parable about a man with two sons. The younger son ran off and foolishly spent all his share of the family fortune. When the money was gone, he was hungry and lonely. He decided to go home and beg his father to forgive him. His loving father welcomed him with great joy. This made the older son jealous and angry. He had stayed home and done just what his father wanted. His father said to him, "Son, you are always with me, and all that is mine is yours. But your brother was lost and now is found. It is time to celebrate!" (15:31-32)

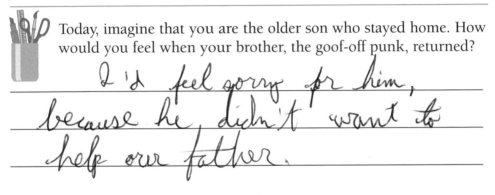

Today, imagine that you are the older son who stayed home. How would you feel when your brother, the goof-off punk, returned?

I'd feel sorry for him, because he didn't want to help our father.

- Do you ever feel jealous of your brother or sister?
- Do you ever feel taken for granted or unappreciated?

Been there? That's okay. But it's not okay to stay there. Try one of these suggestions.

- Congratulate someone who did his or her best at something.
- Thank your parents for something you usually take for granted.

How Much Have You Grown?
Turn to pages 32 and 33. Look at your Promise for Lent. Have you remembered it all week? Think about what you have done this week to grow closer to Jesus. Write it on the leaf.

Did You Know?

The Church year begins with the first Sunday of Advent and ends with the feast of Christ the King. The year is made up of two kinds of time: ordinary and extraordinary (special). Through the cycle of each year, we prepare for and celebrate the two great mysteries of our faith: the Incarnation (God became man) and the Redemption (Jesus saved, or redeemed, us).

The seasons of Advent, Christmas, Lent, and Easter make up the extraordinary times. Between these seasons, we have the Sundays of Ordinary Time. These are not just fill-in Sundays. Their name comes from the old English word *ordinals*, which means "numbered." Each Sunday in Ordinary Time has a number.

In our own lives we have special days, such as birthdays and holidays, along with ordinary days. We have days when we can do big acts of charity, like collecting for a Christmas toy drive. In between, we have ordinary days doing ordinary things, like playing with the baby while dinner is being prepared. Ordinary things are still acts of love as Christ showed us.

One of the ways the Church distinguishes the seasons of the liturgical year is by the colors of vestments, altar cloths, and decorations (see chart below). We have major and minor feasts within each of the liturgical seasons, just as we do in our own lives.

LITURGICAL SEASON	COLOR
Advent • Lent	Violet
Ordinary Time	Green
Christmas • Easter • Holy Thursday	White
Palm Sunday • Good Friday • Feasts of Holy Spirit and of Martyrs	Red
Feasts of Jesus or Mary • Saints who were members of or founders of religious orders • Funeral Masses	White

The Liturgical Year

Unscramble these words associated with the Church seasons.

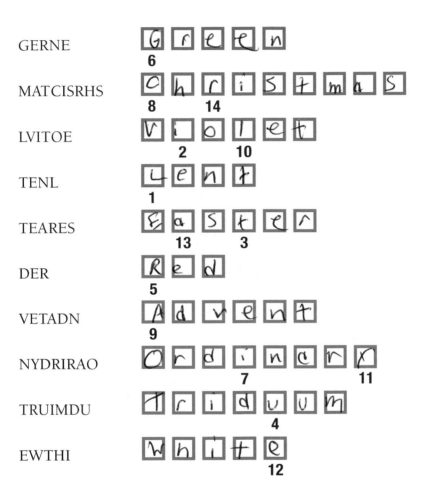

GERNE — G r e e n
6

MATCISRHS — C h r i s t m a s
8 14

LVITOE — V i o l e t
2 10

TENL — L e n t
1

TEARES — E a s t e r
13 3

DER — R e d
5

VETADN — A d v e n t
9

NYDRIRAO — O r d i n a r y
7 11

TRUIMDU — T r i d u u m
4

EWTHI — W h i t e
12

Copy the letters above each number into these boxes.

L i t u r g i c a l   Y e a r
1 2 3 4 5 6 7 8 9 10   11 12 13 14

24 Third Monday of Lent—March 16

Today's Gospel: Luke 4:24-30

They got up, drove Jesus out of town, and led him to a hill so they could hurl him off the cliff. But he passed through their midst and went on his way (4:29-30).

What had made the people so angry at Jesus that they were ready to throw him off a cliff? Jesus was in Nazareth, after all, his own hometown. You'd think the people who had known him all his life would be more willing to listen to him and believe what he said. But that was not the case.

To learn why the people did not accept Jesus' words, replace every letter in this sentence with the letter that comes BEFORE it in the alphabet.

No prophet is
O P   Q S P Q I F U   J T

accepted in
B D D F Q U F E   J O

the prophet's
U I F   Q S P Q I F U T

own land.
P X O   M B O E

Jesus, forgive me when I doubt any of your words. Keep me faithful to you always. Amen.

Today's Gospel: Matthew 18:21-35

Peter asked Jesus, "How often should I forgive? As many as seven times?" Jesus said, "Not seven times, but seventy-seven times" (18:21-22).

Jesus' answer to Peter meant that there is no limit to the number of times we should forgive one another. Forgiveness should multiply, not divide.

 A letter represents the answer to each of these problems. Write the correct letter on the bottom lines on the chalk board and you'll find another thing Jesus wants us to multiply.

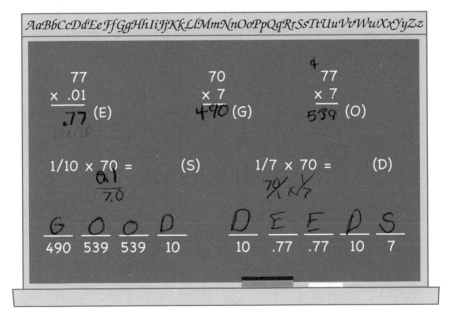

 Today is St. Patrick's day. He is the patron saint of the Irish. Pray this Irish blessing today.

May the road rise to meet you,
May the wind be always at your back,
May the sun shine warm on your face,
May the rains fall soft upon your fields and, until we meet again,
May the Lord hold you in the palm of his hand.

Today's Gospel: Matthew 5:17-19

Jesus was talking to his disciples about following the commandments. He said, "Whoever breaks one of the least of these commandments, and teaches others to do the same, will be called least in the kingdom of heaven; but whoever does them and teaches them will be called great in the kingdom of heaven" (5:19).

What does it mean to be great in the kingdom of heaven? It means to be an active follower of God's word and a teacher, or spreader, of God's peace and justice.

 Imagine that, by your example only, five values (like honesty) will be passed on to the rest of the world. Which values would you choose to live out?

1. _Generosity_
2. _Honesty_
3. _Responsibility_
4. ~~Hope~~ _Faith_
5. _loveing to others_

 Lord, make me an instrument of your peace:
Where there is hatred, let me sow love,
Where there is injury, pardon,
Where there is doubt, faith,
Where there is despair, hope,
Where there is darkness, light,
And where there is sadness, joy.
(Prayer of St. Francis)

21 St. Joseph, Husband of Mary—March 19

Today's Gospel: Matthew 1:16, 18-21, 24a (or) Luke 2:41-51a

All that we know about St. Joseph is in the first chapters of the Gospels of Matthew and Luke. He was Mary's husband and the foster father of Jesus. He was a good, hard-working man who protected his wife and child.

St. Joseph is honored as the patron of many groups. Circle all the groups you think are correct. Then find out if you are right by putting an X through the squares of the grid that you think are NOT part of the answer.

The Church • Families • Workers • Fathers • The Dying • The Poor

%	%	A	Ø	O	L	L	O	%	F	I	T	X	H	E	#	S
~	E	G	@	⟋	◯	R	Y	O	3	U	8	6	P	#	S	2
O	&	F	5	%	P	8	E	$	O	P	+	?	L	@	E	!

St. Joseph is the patron of _All of these groups of people!_

Sharing Bread

Long ago in Italy, a drought caused the crops to fail. People prayed to St. Joseph asking for rain. Their prayers were answered, and they celebrated with a great feast. Through the years, it became the custom on St. Joseph's Day to prepare tables of food for the poor. Many Catholics still observe St. Joseph's Day by baking special breads and sharing them with hungry people. Before your meal today, say this prayer.

Almighty God, the things that grace this table remind us of your many good gifts. Bless this food, and may the prayers of St. Joseph, who provided bread for your son, sustain us on our journey toward your heavenly kingdom. Amen.

Today's Gospel: Mark 12:28-34

"To love God with all the heart, and with all the understanding, and with all the strength, and to love one's neighbor as oneself—this is much more important than all whole burnt offerings and sacrifices" (12:33).

You know the credit card commercial that shows all kinds of neat things you can buy? Then the last thing it shows is something that is "priceless." This was Jesus' message today. Love of God, neighbor, and self are the greatest gifts of all.

Think about each of these gift possibilities. Choose one of them, or write what you think would be a priceless gift. Write or draw your gift of choice inside the box.

IT'S YOUR MOTHER'S BIRTHDAY.
☐ A birthday card, $2.95
☐ A book she wants, $8.95
☐ A box of candy, $12.99
☐ Your priceless gift

framed picture of both of us

YOUR LITTLE BROTHER IS STARTING KINDERGARTEN.
☐ A box of new crayons, $2.95
☐ A back pack, $19.99
☐ A cool new shirt with the school name on it, $14.99
☐ Your priceless gift

a smile every day before school

I love you Lord, my God, with all my heart, soul, mind, and strength. Help me to love my neighbor as you have loved me. Amen.

Third Saturday of Lent—
March 21

Today's Gospel: Luke 18:9-14

Jesus said, "All who exalt themselves will be humbled, but all who humble themselves will be exalted" (18:14).

Today Jesus told the parable about the Pharisee and the tax collector who were praying. The Pharisee boasted loudly that he was better than others, including the tax collector. The tax collector prayed quietly to God to forgive him his sins. Jesus said the tax collector's prayer was more pleasing to God than the Pharisee's.

Notice, however, that Jesus did not say the Pharisee was a bad man. He was not wrong for obeying the law, fasting, and giving money to the poor. He was wrong for bragging about himself and putting the tax collector down.

Did God give you a talent for music or reading or sports? Do you have good health? Are you able to make others laugh? Can you memorize poems and songs? Are you a good organizer? These are just a few of the blessings God may have given you. To write a prayer of thanksgiving for any blessing you have, fill in these blanks. Then pray privately and humbly, acknowledging God's goodness.

Dear Lord,

Thank you for blessing me with a talent for ___*music*___.

    This is how I use that talent to serve others. *Singing to cheer them up*

Thank you for blessing me with an ability to ___*draw*___.

    This is how I use that ability to serve others. *make cards*

Thank you that I am healthy enough to *laugh + joke*.

    This is how I will use that health to serve others. *cheer them up*

Whoever I am, whatever I do, Lord, comes from your goodness. If I fail to remember that or fail to use my gifts well, forgive me, Lord, and help me do better in the future. Amen.

How Much Have You Grown?

Turn to pages 32 and 33. Have you been keeping your Promise for Lent? On the Week 3 space, write one way you have grown closer to Jesus this week.

My Lenten Promise

For Lent, I,

will give up

being mean to

Mrs. and try

to be nicer

to John and Karl

Week 5   Week 4   Week 3   Week 2   Week 1

Week 5
Controling my anger

Week 4
I'm doing well I helped my brother

Week 1
I'm doing OK, but not great

Did You Know?

A traditional Catholic devotion for Lent is the Stations of the Cross. In the Middle Ages, Christians from Europe traveled to the Holy Land. They wanted to see the places they heard about in the Gospels. They wanted to walk where Jesus walked.

When they returned home they made small altars or shrines to remember their travels. Later, these shrines were transferred into their local churches. And that's how we got the Stations of the Cross!

Each station is marked with a cross. Paintings and carvings were added to beautify the churches and to help people pray the stations. There are fourteen official stations, but some books add a fifteenth station for the Resurrection. Read through the Stations of the Cross and think for a few minutes about Christ's journey to his death.

 Jesus is condemned to death.

 Jesus takes up his cross.

 Jesus falls the first time.

 Jesus meets his mother.

 Simon helps Jesus carry his cross.

 Veronica wipes the face of Jesus.

 Jesus falls again.

 The women of Jerusalem comfort Jesus.

 Jesus falls a third time.

 Jesus' clothes are taken away.

 Jesus is nailed to the cross.

 Jesus dies on the cross.

 Jesus is taken down from the cross.

 Jesus is buried in the tomb.

The Stations of the Cross

Look for the Stations of the Cross in your church. Does your church have paintings, carvings, or drawings to enhance the stations? On this page draw a picture of one of the Stations of the Cross.

Jesus picks up his cross

Fourth Monday of Lent—
March 23

Today's Gospel: John 4:43-54

Once a royal official came to Jesus and begged him to come to his home and cure his son, who was near death. Jesus told the man, "Go, your son will live." On his way home, his servants met him on the road and told him that his child's fever broke the day before. It was at the exact time Jesus had told him his son would live (4:46-53).

This all happened a day's journey from the official's home. He had to wait to find out if his son was cured. Sometimes we have to wait for prayers to be answered. Solve this rebus to learn what we need while we wait.

Trust

goat gold God

__Trust__ IN __God__

But I trust in you, O LORD;
*   I say, "You are my God."*
My times are in your hand;
*   deliver me from the hand of*
*   my enemies and persecutors.*
Let your face shine upon your servant;
*   save me in your steadfast love. (Psalm 31:14-16)*

Fourth Tuesday of Lent— March 24

Today's Gospel: John 5:1-16

There was a pool of water in Jerusalem where, people believed, an angel came occasionally and stirred the water. The first one to enter the stirred waters was healed. One man had been ill for thirty-eight years, but he had no one to carry him into the waters. When Jesus saw the man, he said, "Stand up, take your mat and walk" (5:2-9).

Do you know someone who is sick or homebound or in a care facility? Visit, call, or write that person as soon as you can. If you don't know someone you can help, ask a parish minister to deliver the card to a parishioner who is sick or homebound. Remember to pray for the person you visit or contact.

Write a prayer to Jesus, asking him to help you with something you need. Tell Jesus that you trust him. Then don't worry about it another second.

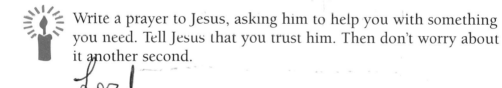

Lord,

Please help me be more organized. I know you'll do what's best for me.

The Annunciation of the Lord— March 25

Today's Gospel: Luke 1:26-38

In the sixth month, the angel Gabriel was sent by God to…a virgin engaged to a man whose name was Joseph. The virgin's name was Mary (1:26-28).

 After you've read today's Gospel, find these words in the puzzle.

COUSIN	JESUS	NAZARETH
ELIZABETH	JOSEPH	MARY
GABRIEL	GRACE	LORD

J	O	S	E	P	H	L	Q	N
E	E	Y	M	Q	L	E	C	A
S	X	C	Y	M	N	I	O	Z
U	Y	J	A	R	P	R	U	A
S	D	R	C	R	B	B	S	R
K	R	T	A	R	G	A	I	E
H	O	Z	C	M	H	G	N	T
E	L	I	Z	A	B	E	T	H
C	X	K	T	N	C	L	H	B

Bring good news to someone today by letting them know that you are with them when they are afraid or facing a difficult time.

 Mary, my model, help me always to respond "Yes" to what God asks of me. Amen.

Today's Gospel: John 5:31-47

Look up the following verses in your Bible. In each of these verses, you will find the word that completes the sentence below.

Deuteronomy 4:29
Psalm 139:23
Jeremiah 17:10

Matthew 2:8
Luke 15:8

Search the Scriptures in which you have eternal life.

Now look up John 5:39 to see if you are right!

Many people who were waiting for the Messiah didn't see Jesus for whom he was. Today, be aware of everyone you meet. How do people show you God's love, mercy, justice, truth, and compassion? Search for the face of God wherever you are—at home, at the mall, in the classroom. Record what you see in the spaces below.

Annie Jo	always cheerful
(Name of person)	(God-like action)
Max	always respectful
(Name of person)	(God-like action)
Karl	has lots of levity
(Name of person)	(God-like action)

Thank you, God, for showing your face to me through my family, friends, classmates, and people who help me. Amen.

Today's Gospel: John 7:1-2, 10, 25-30

Jesus told the people, "The one who sent me is true, and you do not know him" (7:29).

Although Jesus' people had been waiting a very long time for the Messiah, they did not recognize him. Even with all the signs pointing to Jesus, many people ignored the signs or failed to understand them.

 See if you recognize these signs and symbols. Write what each means on the line next to it.

Jesus _____

_____

_____

_____

Peace _____

_____ *New life*

 Psalms are the song prayers of the Jewish people. Jesus learned the psalms when he was your age.

I say to the LORD, "You are my God" (Psalm 140:6).

40

Fourth Saturday of Lent— March 28

Today's Gospel: John 7:40-53

Some in the crowd said, "This is really the prophet." Others said, "This is the Messiah." But some asked, "Surely the Messiah does not come from Galilee, does he?" (7:40-41)

People were judging Jesus without knowing whom he was. Was he the Messiah? Was he a prophet? Besides that, they considered the people from Galilee uneducated and uncool.

How quick are you to judge without knowing the facts? If you hear that a certain kid is stupid, do you give that person a chance or do you accept what other people say?

Think about what you need to be and what you need to do in order to see the best in others. For example, "I need *to be* more patient so I **will** really listen to other people."

Fill in the quality you need.

• I need *to be* more ___gentle___.

Write what you will do to develop that quality.

• I *will* ___not act without thinking___

_____.

🌻 **How Much Have You Grown?**
  Turn to pages 32 and 33. It's time to check on how you are doing. On the leaf by Week 4, write one way you did God's will this week.

Did You Know?

Jelly beans come in many colors and flavors. Do you have a favorite?
This little prayer uses some of the colors of jelly beans to remind us of
Christ's love for us. See if you can fill in the color for each line.

__red__ is for the blood he gave.

__green__ is for the grass he made.

__yellow__ is for the sun so bright.

__purple__ is for the edge of night.

__black__ is for the sins we made.

__white__ is for the grace he gave.

__ __ __ __ __ __ is for his hour of sorrow.

__blue__ is for our new tomorrow.

The Jelly Bean Prayer

Find scraps of construction paper in the same colors as the colors in the Jelly Bean Prayer. Cut small pieces of paper of each color. Use the pieces to make a mosaic in the cross below.

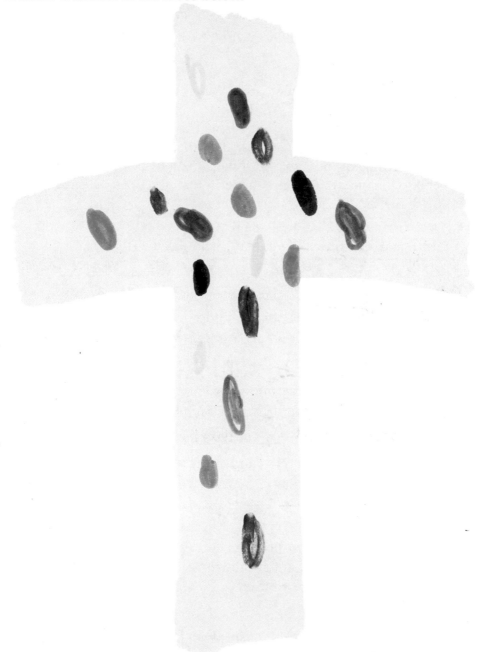

Today's Gospel: John 8:1-11

They brought a woman who was caught in adultery to stand before Jesus. They said, "In the law Moses commanded us to stone such women. What do you say?" Jesus answered, "Let anyone who is without sin be the first to throw a stone" (8:5-7).

Was it right to stone the woman? No. Was it moral? No. Was it legal? Yes, at that time!

 You may think that since those days there have not been laws that were wrong or immoral. Read the situations below. Answer yes or no to the questions. Write the term that describes the situation. Use the Word List if you need help.

1. A white man can buy a black man, who has no rights.

Is it fair?	Is it moral?	Is it legal?	Was it ever legal?	What is this called?
no	no	no	yes	slavery

2. A pregnant woman can choose to end her baby's life.

Is it fair?	Is it moral?	Is it legal?	Was it ever legal?	What is this called?
no	no	yes	yes	abortion

3. Only men can apply for certain jobs.

Is it fair?	Is it moral?	Is it legal?	Was it ever legal?	What is this called?
no	no	no	yes	discrimination

4. In some states all murderers can be put to death.

Is it fair?	Is it moral?	Is it legal?	Was it ever legal?	What is this called?
no	no	y?	yes	

Word List
Discrimination • Capital Punishment •
Abortion • Slavery

Jesus, give me the courage to speak up for what is right.

Fifth Tuesday of Lent—March 31

Today's Gospel: John 8:21-30

Jesus said, "The one who sent me is with me; he has not left me alone, for I always do what is pleasing to him" (8:29).

Jesus knew when his life on this earth would end. And he knew that he had lived as his Father wanted him to live. Take a look at your life so far. Write a short story titled, "Welcome to My Life." Use at least five of these words.

~~comfortable~~	~~loyalty~~	praise
understanding	greatest	~~best~~
~~faith~~	~~thankful~~	~~gift~~
courage	appreciate	~~love~~

Welcome to My Life

I am very thankful for my life. It is the best gift I could be given. I was born on December 5, 1997. I went to a small comfortable preschool from ages 2-5. Then I started going to St. Anne's. At St. Anne's I have gained much more faith. We have taught to show loyalty and love to all.

When I think about my life so far, Lord, I see many blessings you have given me. Thank you for them. Help me to remember my blessings when I start to complain about what I don't have. Amen.

Today's Gospel: John 8:31-42

Jesus said to the Jews who had believed in him, "If you continue in my word, you are truly my disciples, and you will know the truth and the truth will set you free." They answered him, "We are descendants of Abraham and have never been slaves to anyone. What do you mean, 'You will be made free?'" (8:31-33)

The Jews had trouble at times following the meaning of Jesus' words. See if you can follow the words in this squiggle puzzle. They were all in today's Gospel. All of the words squiggle around and about. One of them has been done for you.

Word List
- Abraham
- Father
- Sin
- Disciples
- God
- Jesus
- Jews
- Descendants
- Opportunity
- Son
- Slave

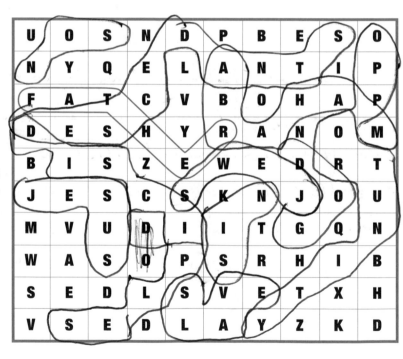

Holy Spirit, give me strength and wisdom.
Help me to stand up for what is right, even when I'm alone.
Help me to stand up with others when they are doing the right thing.

Fifth Thursday of Lent—April 2

Today's Gospel: John 8:51-59

Jesus said, "If I glorify myself, my glory is nothing. It is my Father who glorifies me" (8:54).

Best Effort
School Play
Science
Basketball
Soccer
Music Recital
Math Super Bowl   PEOPLE'S CHOICE   Reader Reward

 When you do something well, do you give credit to God for your talent? You have won a People's Choice award. Write a short acceptance speech.

Thank you for giving me this award, even though I don't deserve it. I know that this talent comes from God.

Blessed Teresa of Calcutta received many awards, including the Nobel Peace Prize, for her work with the poorest people in India. She said, "By serving the poor, I am serving Jesus."

Jesus, help me to do ordinary things with extraordinary love. Amen.

Today's Gospel: John 10:31-42

Jesus said, "If I am not doing the works of my Father, then do not believe me. But if I do them, even though you do not believe me, believe the works, so that you may know and understand that the Father is in me and I am in the Father" (10:37-38).

These people all put their faith into action during their lives. Match each person with his or her good works. (Hint: You've already read about these people in this book.)

1. St. Frances of Rome ___e___

2. St. Joseph ___e___

3. St. Katherine Drexel ___a___

4. St. Basil ___d___

5. St. Patrick ___b___

a. Although wealthy, this person lived a life sacrificing for others, building schools and missions for African Americans and Native Americans in the USA.

b. This person is the patron saint of the Irish. Many who are not Irish celebrate his feast day, too.

c. On this person's feast day, special breads are baked and blessed and shared with the poor.

d. This person said, "The bread you do not use is the bread of the hungry."

e. When the river flooded, this wealthy person opened a soup kitchen and invited the homeless to live in a palace.

My God, I believe that you are one God in three persons—Father, Son, and Holy Spirit. Help me to tell others about you through my words and my actions. Amen.

7 Fifth Saturday of Lent—April 4

Today's Gospel: John 11:45-56

Many of the Jews who saw what Jesus did believed in him. But some went to the Pharisees and told them what he had done. So the chief priests and Pharisees called a meeting of the council and said, "What are we to do? This man is performing many signs. If we let him go on like this, the whole world will believe in him" (11:45-48).

 The enemies of Jesus were able to stop him, but they couldn't stop his message. Design a billboard that shows others you believe in Jesus.

How Much Have You Grown?
Turn to pages 32 and 33. Don't give up on your promise now. On the Week 5 space, write one way that you have been a sign of God's love to your friends.

49

Did You Know?

In our lives we have good times and bad times. During Holy Week we remember some of the good and bad times in Christ's life. With other Christians, we walk, watch, and wait for Easter. During this time, the liturgy of the Church helps us get in touch with the experiences of Jesus. Next to each liturgical action, write which of your five senses—sight, hearing, smell, taste, touch—helps you understand or recognize it.

Waving palms _____ *sight* _____

Singing Hosanna _____ *hear* _____

Bells ringing _____ *hear* _____

Covered statues _____ *sight* _____

Receiving Eucharist _____ *taste* _____

Stripping of the altar _____ *sight* _____

Venerating the cross _____ *sight* _____

Blessing with baptismal waters _____ *touch* _____

Incensing the altar _____ *smell* _____

Lighting the new fire _____ *sight* _____

Blessing of the oils _____ *smell* _____

Hosanna

Holy Week

Draw a road from the high of Palm Sunday to the low of Good Friday and back to the high of Easter.

The highest holy day is Easter. We celebrate the resurrection of Jesus. By rising, Jesus conquered sin and death forever.

Palm Sunday marks the triumphant entrance of Christ into Jerusalem. We celebrate with processions, palm branches, and joyous songs.

Holy Saturday is a time of waiting for Christ to be freed from the tomb and to be with us again.

Holy Thursday marks the institution of the Eucharist. We thank God for the Living Bread that nourishes us on our journey.

On Good Friday we walk the road to Calvary where Christ died for our sins.

Monday of Holy Week—April 6

Today's Gospel: John 12:1-11

Jesus had just finished eating a meal at the home of his friends, Mary, Martha, and Lazarus. Mary brought in a pound of expensive perfume and gently rubbed it onto Jesus' feet. The spicy fragrance filled the whole house. The perfume was worth at least 300 silver pieces! (12:1-5)

Mary held nothing back out of love for Jesus. Soon Jesus will give his life on the cross. He will hold nothing back out of love for you.

Do you ever hold back when you have a chance to show your love for Jesus?

Answer each of these questions honestly.

During Mass, do you sing out as best as you can, or do you barely move your lips?

I sing

When someone uses Jesus' name irreverently, do you ignore it, or do you ask the person not to speak that way when with you?

I ignore it, but pray about it

If someone is sick or hurting, do you offer to pray with or for the person, or do you just say, "Good luck"?

pray

Lord Jesus, when I see the chance to show my love for you, help me to go for it. When I get the chance to serve others with love, help me to go for it. Amen.

Today's Gospel: John 13:21-33, 36-38

Peter said to Jesus, "Lord, I will lay down my life for you." Jesus answered, "Will you lay down your life for me? Very truly, I tell you, before the cock crows, you will have denied me three times" (13:37-38).

Peter's heart was in the right place. He just didn't have the courage right then to follow through. When the rooster crowed, Peter woke up to what he had done. Who is the rooster that crows for you? It could be any of these.

- A friend confronts you about your actions.

- A teacher gives you detention for not doing your home work.

- A parent grounds you for breaking house rules.

- A coach benches you for missing practice.

Who is the rooster that crows for you?

• a friend confronts you about your actions

Are you ever the rooster that crows for someone else? In what way?

• Sometimes I tell my brothers to stop fighting

Later, with the help of the Holy Spirit, Peter more than made up for his triple denial of Jesus. Say this prayer to the Holy Spirit.

Come, Holy Spirit, fill my heart with understanding. Help me to hear the people who speak up when I am headed in the wrong direction.
Come, Holy Spirit, fill my heart with courage. Help me to make better choices.
Come, Holy Spirit, let the fire of your love burn away my selfishness and fear. Amen.

53

Wednesday of Holy Week—
April 8

Today's Gospel: Matthew 26:14-25

Jesus told his apostles, "I tell you, one of you will betray me." They began to say to him one after another, "Surely not I, Lord?" (26:21-22)

If you were there, would you be saying, "Is it I, Lord?" The truth is that we all betray Jesus in some way.

- By refusing to include someone in our group
- By not using his name with respect
- By not paying attention at Mass
- By not obeying those in authority

All of our denials and betrayals put Jesus on the cross. And Jesus forgave all of our denials and betrayals while he was on the cross.

Trace the cross on this page onto cardboard. Cut out the cardboard cross. Spread glue on the surface of the cross. Starting at the center, wrap cord or yarn in loops, gluing it down as you go, until you have covered the whole cross.

Each time you make a loop on your cross, tell Jesus you are sorry for the times you betrayed him.

I just stayed quiet when my brothers were fighting. I didn't stand up for my faith this summer.

Oh, my Jesus, forgive me my sins. Save me from the fires of hell. Lead all souls to heaven, especially those most in need of your mercy. Amen.

3 Holy Thursday—April 9

Today's Gospel: John 13:1-15

Jesus said to his apostles, "So if I, your Lord and Teacher, have washed your feet, you also ought to wash one another's feet" (13:14).

Jesus teaches us to serve all people even in situations as dirty and stinky as washing feet. Think of a chore around the house that no one likes to do, such as cleaning the bathroom. Do this chore without being asked.

The Spirit is willing, but the flesh is weak.

After eating the Passover supper with the apostles, Jesus went to the Garden of Gethsemane to pray. He took Peter, James, and John with him. Read Mark 14:32-41.

Tonight, celebrate the Mass of the Lord's Supper at church. Afterward, spend some quiet time with Jesus in the Blessed Sacrament. Don't fall asleep like the apostles did!

Triduum Facts—Holy Thursday

The oils used in the sacraments of Baptism, Confirmation, Holy Orders, and Anointing of the Sick are blessed at the cathedral in your diocese and brought back to your parish.

We celebrate the institution of the Eucharist at the Last Supper. The Eucharist nourishes you on your journey through life. The love and grace you receive in the Eucharist gives you the strength to wash feet, as Jesus did.

There is no dismissal to the Mass on Holy Thursday. We leave in silence to show the unity of the Triduum or Three Days: Holy Thursday, Good Friday, and Easter.

Today's Gospel: John 18:1—19:42

Carrying the cross by himself, he went out to what is called The Place of the Skull, which in Hebrew is called Golgotha (19:16-17).

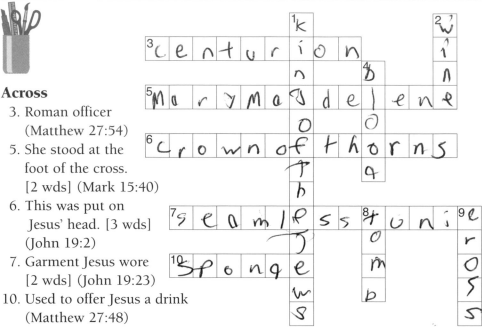

Across

3. Roman officer (Matthew 27:54)
5. She stood at the foot of the cross. [2 wds] (Mark 15:40)
6. This was put on Jesus' head. [3 wds] (John 19:2)
7. Garment Jesus wore [2 wds] (John 19:23)
10. Used to offer Jesus a drink (Matthew 27:48)

Down

1. Title used by soldiers to mock Jesus [4 wds] (Luke 23:37)
2. A sour drink offered to Jesus (Luke 23:36)
4. Mixed with water, this poured from Jesus' side. (John 19:34)
8. Where Jesus' body was laid (Luke 23:53)
9. What Jesus carried (John 19:17)

Triduum Facts—Good Friday

† Good Friday is the only day of the year when there is no Mass. We have a Communion service but not a Mass. The hosts we use for Communion are reserved from Mass on Holy Thursday.

Holy Saturday—April 11

Today's Gospel: John 19:38-42

The Scripture readings for the Easter Vigil cover the history of our salvation, from when God created the world to when Jesus came to redeem us. It is the story of God's love for us.

Look up each Scripture reading and note the major events or people in our salvation history.

Genesis 1:1—2:2 _Worlds creation_

Genesis 22:1-18 _Abraham offers Isaac_

Exodus 14:15—15:1 _Moses splits the Red Sea_

Isaiah 54:5-14 _God promises safety to his chosen people._

Isaiah 55:1-11 _God promises safety to his chosen people._

Baruch 3:9-15, 32—4:4 _Israelites turn away from God_

Ezekiel 36:16-28 _Israelites are scattered_

Triduum Facts—Easter Vigil

The water used in Baptism is blessed. This water washes us and gives us life in Christ. Each time you enter church, sign yourself with the baptismal water and remember your place in God's family.

Fire is also blessed and carried into church. It reminds us that Christ is our light. At Baptism and at Easter Vigil, we light a candle from the Easter Candle. This reminds us that it is our responsibility to bring Christ's light to the world.

How Will You Keep Growing?

Turn to pages 32 and 33. For Week 6, write one of the ways you have grown closer to Jesus during Lent.

Did You Know?

The liturgy of Easter Vigil begins with lighting a fire, usually outside the church. The new fire is used to light a large candle called the Paschal Candle.

The word *Paschal* comes from the Jewish word for Passover. The Paschal Candle represents Christ, the Light of the World. The lighted candle is a sign that Jesus overcomes the darkness of sin and death.

On the next page is the outline of a candle. Decorate it like this:

- **In the middle of the candle, draw a cross.**

- **At the top of the candle, make the Greek letter Alpha.**

 Alpha is the first letter of the Greek alphabet. It shows that Jesus is the Beginning of everything.

- **At the bottom of the candle, make the Greek letter Omega.**

 Omega is the last letter of the Greek alphabet. It shows that Jesus is the End of everything.

- **Put one red dot at the end of each line of the cross.**
  These are for the four wounds in Jesus' head, hands, and feet.

- **Put one red dot at the center of the cross.**
  This is for the wound in Jesus' side.

- **In the four corners of the cross, write the numbers of the year.**

- **Draw a flame on the candle and color it.**

 May the light of Christ, rising in glory, dispel the darkness of our hearts and minds. Amen.

The Paschal Candle

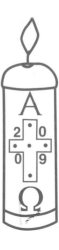

Easter Sunday—April 12

Today's Gospel: John 20:1-9

Early on the first day of the week, while it was still dark, Mary Magdalene came to the tomb and saw that the stone had been removed (20:1).

Do you remember where you "buried" the *Alleluia* way back at the beginning of Lent? It's time to bring it out! On Easter morning we again sing **Alleluia!**

Do you remember what *Alleluia* means? Find the correct path through this maze. Write each letter in that path on the lines below. Be careful. Some paths are misleading.

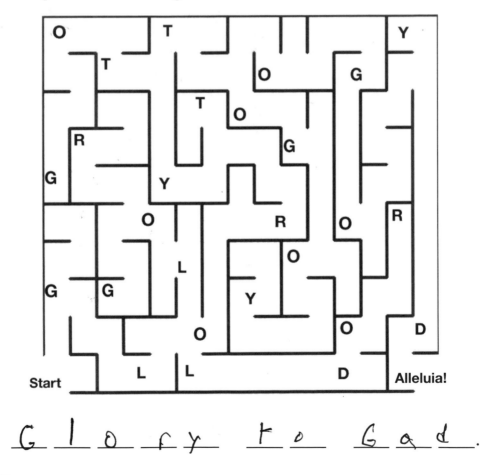

G l o r y   t o   G o d.

Write a joyful Easter phrase using each letter of the word *Alleluia*.

Example:

DANCE AND SING
ALL CREATURES of the EARTH
For the LORD IS RISEN
This EASTER DAY.
LIFT UP your VOICES
With SHOUTS of JOY
For CHRIST LIVES
And WE ARE FREED from DEATH.

Try it!

Celebr Ate
Be G Lad
The L ord
is Ris En
L ife is renewed
U nstoppable love
Lent I s over
A lleluia!

Jesus told Mary Magdalene to go tell the brothers. (See Matthew 28:9–10.) With whom do you you share good news?

Jesus showed his friends that he was still with them. He said, "peace be with you." (See John 20:19–20.) When do you feel peaceful?

After Jesus died, the apostles were alone and scared. (See Mark 16:8.) When do you feel like that?

GO FORTH!

My family!

When I'm reading

When I feel like that?

When I melt new people.

Working from the inside out, answer each question.
Write in the middle space and the spaces between questions.

Jesus promised to be with us always. (See Matthew 28:20.) How can you continue to grow closer to Jesus?

Where do you take the spirit of Jesus?

Read the Bible

Jesus sent the apostles out into the world to teach others about him. (See Matthew 28:20.) What questions do you have for Jesus?

To the softball field

Jesus explained the Scriptures on the road to Emmaus. (See Luke 24:27.)

GO FORTH!

How did you put up with so much pain?

Working from the inside out, answer each question.
Write in the middle space and the spaces between questions.

Answers

Page 4: 1. B; 2. A; 3. B; 4. A; 5. A; 6. B

Page 7:
1. sack; 2. rah; 3. meant; 4. of; 5a. wreck;
5b. con; 5c. sill; 5d. e; 5e. shun
Answer: The Sacrament of Reconciliation.

Page 12: Something greater than Jonah is here.

Page 13: 4=O; 7=E; 5=L; 0=T; 1=H; 10=U;
12=E; 3=G; 2=E; 9=R; 11=L; 6=D; 8=N. The Golden Rule

Page 15: Be perfect as your heavenly Father is perfect.

Page 18:

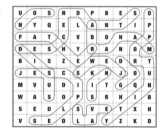

Page 20: Whoever wishes to be first among you must be your servant.

Page 22: justice; kindness; peace; love; charity; goodness; hope; joy; faith; patience

Page 25: green; Christmas; violet; Lent; Easter; red; Advent; Ordinary; Triduum; white. **Answer:** Liturgical Year

Page 26: No prophet is accepted in the prophet's own land.

Page 27: Good deeds.

Page 29: All of these groups of people.

Page 36: TRUCK – CK + NEST + T – NET = TRUST
GOAT + EN – TEN – A + L + DOG – LOG = GOD

Page 38:

Page 39: Search

Page 40: fish=Christian; shell=Baptism; cross=crucifixion or Jesus; bread and wine= Eucharist; dove=Holy Spirit; butterfly= Resurrection

Page 42: red; green; yellow; orange; black; white; purple; pink

Page 44: 1. slavery; 2. abortion; 3. discrimination; 4. capital punishment

Page 46:

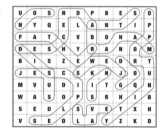

Page 48: 1. E; 2. C; 3. A; 4. D; 5. B

Page 56: Across: 3. centurion; 5. Mary Magdalene; 6. crown of thorns; 7. seamless tunic; 10. sponge
Down: 1. King of the Jews; 2. wine; 4. blood; 8. tomb; 9. cross

Page 60:

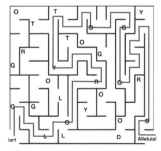

Answer: Glory to God